Ants, Bees, and Other Social Insects

By Kris Hirschmann

World Discovery Science Readers™

SCHOLASTIC INC.

New York • Toronto • London • Auckland • Sydney
Mexico City • New Delhi • Hong Kong • Buenos Aires

Black ants swarming.

Chapter 1

Insect Society

A big pile of dirt sits on the jungle floor. Nothing moves on the dirt's surface. But there is a lot of activity inside the pile. Millions of ants are crawling over one another. They are eating, taking care of eggs, and building tunnels. They are living together as a **colony**.

Insects that form colonies are called **social insects**. There are four types of social insects: ants, termites, wasps, and bees. All ants and termites are social. Most wasps and bees are **solitary**, which means they live alone. Only a few types form colonies.

There are about a million known species of insects. Less than two percent of these species are social. This graph compares solitary and social species.

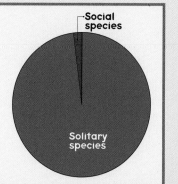

Social species

Solitary species

Termites

Some insect colonies are huge. A termite colony may contain millions of bugs. The biggest colonies are in Africa.

Ants also form very large colonies. Millions of ants may share an entire underground nest. Most big ant colonies are in Africa and the Amazon rain forest of South America. Imagine you could weigh all the ants in these areas on one giant scale. Then imagine weighing all of these areas' remaining animals on another scale. The ants would be heavier!

Ants

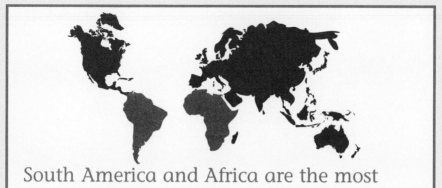

South America and Africa are the most ant-infested parts of the world.

Social bees and wasps form smaller colonies. The biggest groups of honeybees have about 80,000 insects. Most wasp colonies have just a few hundred members.

Bees

Wasps

5

Black ants and queen

Each insect in a colony has a special job. The most important job belongs to the **queen**. The queen does nothing but lay eggs. African driver ant queens can lay more than 100,000 eggs in one day! Termite queens lay up to 30,000 eggs per day, and honeybee queens may lay 2,000 eggs each day.

This termite queen's **abdomen** is swollen with eggs.

The other insects in a colony are called **workers**. They are much smaller than queens. Some workers bring food to the queen and take care of her eggs until they hatch. Other workers take care of the newly hatched insects, which are called **larvae**. Workers also repair the nest. The rest of the workers guard the colony or go out each day to look for food.

Red worker ants tend larvae.

Bee gathering pollen for food.

Queen bee in hive

Most bee and termite colonies have just one queen. A healthy queen makes a **chemical** that spreads through the colony. This chemical tells the workers to stop new queens from hatching.

Very old or sick queens cannot make enough of the chemical to reach every worker. When this happens, workers start giving special food to some larvae. The food turns the young insects into queens. The strongest queen takes over the old queen's job.

Sometimes new queens hatch because a colony has become too big. The young queens leave the colony, taking thousands of older workers with them. The groups soon find homes and start building brand-new colonies. Ants often build new colonies right next to old ones.

New colony constructs its hive.

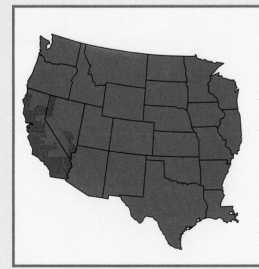

Groups of ant colonies are called **supercolonies**. This map shows the size and shape of an ant supercolony in Califonia and Nevada.

Black ants

Chapter 2

How Insects Talk

It takes a lot of work to run an insect colony. Tasks like finding food and fixing the nest must be done every single day. The colony would fail if each insect did not do its part.

How do insects know what to do? They **communicate** with one another through smells, sounds, and motions. The information they trade keeps the colony running smoothly.

An insect's **antennae** are covered with tiny hairs that sense motion and odors.

Ants following trail.

All social insects use smell and sound to help them communicate. Smell is especially important to ants. These insects put down trails of stinky liquid that lead to food. Have you ever seen a line of ants marching one after the other? They are following the invisible **scent trail** created by another ant.

The chemical scent, also called **pheromone**, that ants use is very strong. A drop of it that is this big could lead a line of ants around the world several times. ⟶ ●

Ants and other social insects trade other types of information through smell, too. For example, they can ask other insects to help them do things. They can tell other insects to follow them. And they can spread a danger signal through the colony.

Sound is also important to insects. Some ants make squeaks or tapping sounds to send messages to one another. Some wasps, including the mud dauber wasp, make a buzzing noise with their wings to "speak" to other wasps.

Mud dauber wasp

Bees communicate to lead one another to pollen.

Bees have an amazing way of communicating. They dance to lead one another to food! A worker bee that has found food returns to the colony. She buzzes to attract other bees. Then she begins to dance. She takes several steps forward, waggling her abdomen as she walks. She points her body toward the food source. She also walks in circles that show the distance to the food source. She repeats this over and over again.

This diagram shows a bee's **waggle dance**. The middle line points to the food. The outer lines communicate distance.

Other bees watch the dance carefully. Sometimes they touch the dancer with their antennae to get more information. Soon they learn how to reach the food. They fly straight to the food source without making any mistakes.

Paper wasps begin to construct their nest.

Chapter 3

Home Sweet Home

Social insects are natural builders. They work together to construct a home for the colony. They make the home bigger and bigger over time.

Insect homes start out simple, but they get more complicated as they grow. A big insect home has many different parts that are used for different things.

What types of homes do social insects build?

This swarm of bees is looking for a new home.

Some types of termites build large, rock-hard **mounds**. Termite mounds can be more than 20 feet (6.1 m) high! They are made of soil bits. The termites use their sticky spit to glue the bits together.

A mound has many rooms and passages. Some of the rooms are nurseries where termite eggs hatch. Other rooms are living chambers or places to store food. Some termites even plant fungus gardens inside their mounds.

Termites live in the soil beneath the mounds, too. The underground part of the nest is bigger than the mound.

A termite mound acts like an air conditioner. Heat escapes from the top of the mound. Holes in the mound's sides let cool air come in. Most termites that build mounds live in hot areas, such as the deserts of Africa and Australia. So this cooling system is very important.

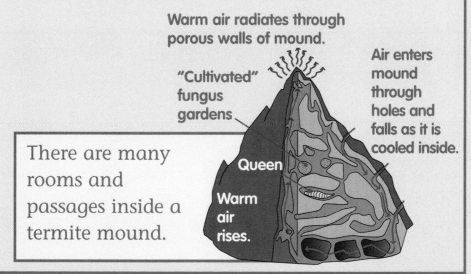

Warm air radiates through porous walls of mound.

"Cultivated" fungus gardens

Air enters mound through holes and falls as it is cooled inside.

Queen

Warm air rises.

There are many rooms and passages inside a termite mound.

Ants build many different types of homes. Red ants often make nests in rotten tree stumps. Every day they dump little bits of grass, leaves, and other materials around the stump. Over time this matter piles up and makes a soft mound for the ants to live in.

Ants may also dig nests inside tree branches and plant stems. Plants swell as ants damage them. Swollen parts on a stem show that insects live inside it.

Ant hill

Weaver ants make homes out of leaves. An adult weaver ant holds a larva in its jaws. It moves the larva back and forth, touching its head to different leaves.

Weaver ants join leaves together to create a nest

The larva makes sticky silk strands as it moves. The strands "sew" the leaves together into rooms.

13 feet

13 feet Some ants dig nests more than 13 feet (4 m) deep.

Bees and wasps are also skilled builders. The hard outer wall of a **beehive** is made from tree sap mixed with other matter. **Honeycombs** hang inside the hive. Bees build the honeycombs with wax that they scrape from their bodies.

Bee and wasp cells are **hexagonal** (six sided). A nest or hive may hold thousands of cells.

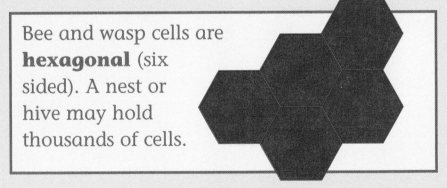

Bees fill honeycomb cells with honey.

Some **cells** of a honeycomb hold bee eggs or larvae. Other cells are used to store pollen and honey. The bees eat the pollen and honey when they cannot find food outside the beehive.

Some wasps make cells, too. Wasps build their cells out of paper. They make the paper by chewing tiny pieces of dead wood into a gooey **pulp**. Wasps use their legs to pat the pulp into the proper shape.

Chapter 4

Working Together

Social insects do not just live together. They also work together to get things done. Jobs that one insect could not do are easy when many work together.

Finding food and defending the colony are two of the most important group activities. Thousands of insects help with these tasks.

Bees carry pollen on their back legs. A single bee cannot carry much pollen. But a group of bees can gather lots of food.

Army ant

Social insects have many ways to find the food they need. South American army ants are **predators** that hunt and eat other animals. Up to 500,000 army ants may hunt as a group. The swarm marches through the jungle looking for mammals or insects. They bite their prey and inject poison to paralyze it. Working together, army ants can eat large animals such as birds and pigs.

Termites also work together to eat large objects. Wood is the termite's favorite meal. A big termite colony can eat a dead tree within days. Sometimes termites also eat the wooden parts of people's houses.

Termites eating wood.

A termite colony can do a lot of damage to a house.

Other insects **cooperate** to grow food. Leafcutter ants, for example, plant a special fungus inside their nests. Many ants tend the gardens to keep the fungus growing.

Leafcutter ants

The search for food can start wars among insects. Hornets, which are a type of wasp, sometimes send groups to attack honeybee hives. The hornets kill the bees by biting them. Then they carry the dead bees back to their nest. They feed the bees to their larvae.

Black ants struggle over food.

Ants also attack other insects. Groups of ants sometimes enter termite colonies and kill all the termites they can catch. Ants also attack wasp colonies. They even go to war against other ant colonies.

Yellow jacket wasp

A formicine ant overpowering a termite soldier.

Social insects defend themselves if they are attacked. Bees, wasps, and some ants use their sharp stingers for this purpose. Some species can inject poison with their stingers. Some, like the common garden ant, can even squirt acid from their abdomens.

Termites do not have stingers. But they do have strong jaws that can tear apart other insects. Some termites also spray a sticky liquid that glues attackers to the floor so they cannot move.

A bee's stinger is lined with barbs. The barbs make it hard to remove the stinger from flesh.

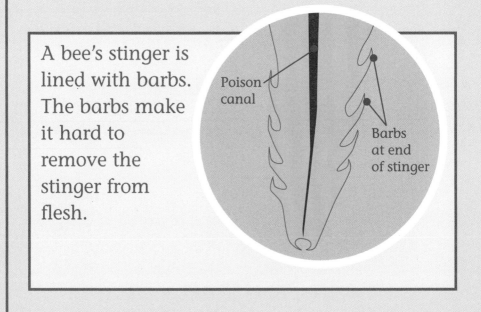

Poison canal

Barbs at end of stinger

Fire ants

Social insects can also defend themselves against large animals. They attack as a group to scare away the animal. Bees and wasps land all over their enemy and sting until it goes away. Fire ants crawl onto the enemy and bite it thousands of times.

Group defense is one reason social insects are so successful. Working together has helped these amazing insects survive for more than 100 million years. They will probably survive far into the future.

Fossilized Bee

Glossary

Abdomen: The rear part of an insect's body.

Antennae: [an-TEN-ee] Organs on an insect's head that taste, smell, and sense motion.

Beehive: A bee colony's home.

Cell: One segment of a honeycomb or a wasp nest.

Chemicals: The basic building blocks of all matter. Everything is made of chemicals.

Colony: A group of insects living together.

Communicate: To share information or ideas.

Cooperate: To work together.

Hexagonal: Six sided.

Honeycomb: A waxy sheet with cells to store food, eggs, and other materials. Honeycombs are built by bees.

Larvae: [LARV-ee] What insects are called right after they hatch.

Mound: A termite colony's home.

Pheromone: [FAIR-uh-mohn] A chemical scent creatures use to communicate with one another through smell.

Predators: Animals that hunt and eat other animals.

Pulp: Soft, chewed-up wood.

Queen: The insect that lays all the eggs.

Scent trail: A line of smell laid down by ants to lead one another to food.

Social insects: Insects that live together in colonies.

Solitary: Living by itself.

Supercolonies: Groups of ant colonies.

Waggle dance: A bee dance that tells others where to find food.

Workers: Insects that do jobs other than laying eggs.